Successfully Navigating High School

A Guide for Students Entering
High School and Their Parents,
Because the Path to Graduating
with Honors Begins in Ninth Grade

Anita Tucker Baxter

Successfully Navigating High School
A Guide for Students Entering High School and Their Parents, Because
the Path to Graduating with Honors Begins in Ninth Grade

Anita Tucker Baxter

DEDICATION

I dedicate this work to my husband and my children who
so often took second place to my students.

TABLE OF CONTENTS

ACKNOWLEDGMENTS

I acknowledge all of my wonderful students; you never believed me, but I loved every one of you. Thank you also to the skilled professionals I have been privileged to work with.

Introduction

I remember bringing my first child home from the hospital, a squirming, screaming mass of eating, sleeping, and pooping. Five minutes later, we were moving her into her college dorm. It's a vapor. You think you have plenty of time to make decisions. You don't. You think, "It'll all be Ok." It will. No matter how responsibly or irresponsibly you plan for your child's future, it will, eventually be "OK." What you have to ask yourself is, "Can I make it better?" The answer is yes, yes, you can. You can make it better, easier, less stressful just by taking a few steps along the way. Like everything else in life, a little planning now makes everything go more smoothly later.

In my thirty year plus career in the classroom, I've taught more than two dozen valedictorians and salutatorians. I'm not certain that I've taught them much, but I am absolutely certain that they taught me a great deal. I also spent several years with the students at the other end of the spectrum. I've sat with students the morning of graduation, hoping to pull the last minute "Hail Mary" that would allow them to squeak across the stage. Finally, and I think most importantly, I have also learned one or two things as a Mom, as I helped my own three children persevere through thirteen years of public school. I'd like to share my experience with you.

Good students do things differently than mediocre students, and very differently than poor students. What kind of student will your child be? Students, what kind of student are you?

I don't have all the answers, but I think I can help.....

Successfully Navigating High School
A Guide for Students Entering High School and Their Parents, Because
the Path to Graduating with Honors Begins in Ninth Grade

CHAPTER 1

WHAT EVERY PARENT AND EVERY STUDENT SHOULD KNOW, EVERY YEAR OF HIGH SCHOOL

Decisions

The one thing I can remember saying to my children over and over again when they were younger and off to school was, "Make good choices." As I've grown older and more experiences myself, I think I've learned that making good choices is the only thing. Recently, in Sunday School our teacher asked the rhetorical question, "How many choices do you think we make in a day?" Never having met a rhetorical question I didn't like, I asked my friend Mr. Google. According to his source, the average American makes 35, 000 choices a day. If he's even close to being correct, that's over 30,000 chances to do the right thing, or to go down an irrevocable path.

That's how I'd like to advise my students to look at their education. Your education is not one big decision to do well. It's thousands and thousands of little decisions each and every day that make the big difference in the end. That's true of your education as well of every corner of your life.

Successfully Navigating High School
A Guide for Students Entering High School and Their Parents, Because
the Path to Graduating with Honors Begins in Ninth Grade

Organization

When you're in elementary school, your teacher sends home notes to your parents and imposes folders and color coordination on you. In middle school, there is some of that. In high school, there is little of that. This is incredibly ironic to me, because high school is where students really need a structured organizational system.

The most successful students I've seen, write things down. Students who struggle to catch up at the end of the grading cycles seldom do. Most students make some effort to remember assignments. They take a photograph of the assignment with their phones. They jot the assignment on a piece of notebook paper. They write it on their hand. The most successful students, however, consistently have assignment books, calendars. It seems that they would use electronic devices, doesn't it? The best of the best, use both. They write the assignment in their calendar. They check it off when they turn it in. They turn assignments in early when allowed. They seem to take great satisfaction in turning the assignment in and checking it off their "to-do" list. When do we begin the habits that will allow us to be successful in high school and beyond? We begin now.

Another good idea we can take into high school from elementary school is the homework folder. What if every period a student brought out his homework folder? What if he put the items he needs to complete on the right, and removes the items he completed last night from the left and turns them in to his teacher. What if he did this every period, every day? What if every night he brought out his homework folder and examined the items in the right hand pocket. What if seeing them encouraged him to complete them? The kids who sit on the front row at the graduation ceremony aren't always the smartest kids in the room. Often they're not. What are they? They're the ones who persevered, the ones who turned in something every day, every day, every day. Many times life is like that also. The winners are the ones who show up, who most of the time give their all, but always give something. Winning, being successful, is a habit. Make the habit.

Writing down obligations also, just seems like a good idea, for a middle school student, a high school student, a college student, a professional....it just seems to be a habit of people who live productively. When do I learn how? Now. Start now. Parents, insist that your children engage in this habit. You're the boss. Don't laugh. Remember when your child was in elementary school and you checked the notebook? Teach your teenager to parent himself. Teach him to check his own notebook, his assignment folder, his list, his calendar every day. If he begins to do poorly, you may have to intervene, but remember the ultimate goal, a grown up, leaving your house, earning a living, doing something he enjoys. Organization and responsibility are something we learn in school that has universal implications into every corner of our lives.

Successfully Navigating High School
A Guide for Students Entering High School and Their Parents, Because
the Path to Graduating with Honors Begins in Ninth Grade

Be Prepared.

Live Your Life on Purpose.

When I was a little girl, growing up in East Texas, I would frequently get in skirmishes with my brother, younger by three years. Before he grew to be a foot taller than I, I'm afraid that I wasn't the best of sisters. It was not unknown for blows to be exchanged. (This is my sad, ashamed face.) Almost always, when my mother intervened, I would use the pitiful excuse, "it was an accident." Come on, really? Truthfully, sometimes it was. Sometimes in the exuberance of youth, I would accidentally strike out and my younger brother would receive a glancing blow. Other times, I was angry at his constant haranguing, or some violence he had perpetrated upon Barbie or her friends, and I would draw back my arm, aim for him, and avenge Barbie with all the force available to me.

Which blow do you think was more substantial? The glancing 'oops' or the carefully aimed strike. The answer is too obvious to discuss. My question to you is are you approaching your high school education as an attendant, necessary evil? You'll go to class, but if you learn something, it is going to be an accident, an incidental, something that comes, because you happen to be in a desk, in the room, not something you sought or planned. Who do you think will be more successful? The one I just described or the one who comes into class, planning to learn, already having a pretty good idea of what to expect for the day? Now here's the hard question, which one are you? Here's the more important question, which one will you be tomorrow? Live your life on purpose.

Studying, being prepared, living life on purpose, it's important.

One of the most talented students I've been privileged to teach, Logan Brown, a graduate of Baylor University had this to say his senior year of college,

"I've sat staring at my computer screen for hours. I was tasked with writing a paragraph on what separates successful students from not so successful students by a former teacher of mine. Easy. I'll write about how success is a direct result of hard work and dedication and that's how I became a successful student. It's summer, I'm a college senior, my friends are in the other room watching a movie I've wanted to see forever, so I'll write it, be done in ten minutes, and join my friends. It's not for a grade and my teacher will be appreciative of anything I give her, even if it is sub-par, so it really doesn't mean that much if it isn't perfect. Yet, I've been staring at this computer screen for hours. I've written the run of the mill success comes from hard work draft ten times, read through them all, ten times, and none of them are good enough. I don't have to spend any time writing this to ensure quality. I don't have to take time away from my friends revising. I don't even have to be writing this right now, but I want to, and that makes all the difference. I wanted to be a successful student, so, like spending time and effort writing this paragraph that has no impact on my life, I did whatever I felt necessary to become that successful student. I truly believe that you can be anything you really want to be. Being a successful student is no different. All successful students want to be successful students and act on those ambitions to bring them to fruition.

Thank you, Logan. You're right, I would have

Successfully Navigating High School
A Guide for Students Entering High School and Their Parents, Because
the Path to Graduating with Honors Begins in Ninth Grade

appreciated anything, but you gave me gold. Logan knows all about gold. Logan Brown was a member of the 2014 Rawlings ABCA Division I Gold Glove Team, not to mention 2014 Academic All-Big 12 First Team, and one of my favorite people.

And parents, Logan graduated got a really good job and got married.

THE ELECTRONIC GRADEBOOK

Technology is a wonderful thing and most school districts now have one form or another of an electronic grade book. Every parent and every student should have an account on the electronic grade book. The days of waiting three weeks for progress reports to see if your teacher has math skills adequate to correctly average your grades are over. You can now see in real time as your teacher enters your grades and if he or she does so correctly. If there is a mistake, you can immediately bring this to your teacher's attention. Most teachers didn't wake up in the morning and drive to school with the intention of robbing his or her students of points earned. If there is a mistake, it's most probably just that, a mistake, and will be readily addressed.

In addition, most electronic grade book systems give the parents and students the ability to receive automatic notifications. You may be notified if you are failing. But why wait until then? If the system will allow you to set the limits, set the notification average high. Have the grade book notify you if your average is less than 115. If a student is successful, congratulations are in order, especially self-congratulations. Setting the notifications to notify only for failure seems defeating to me. Is that really our standard? Is that the one we want to maintain? Perhaps that is the vision we have for our child. "It's Ok that you don't have a good job, honey, as long as you're not below the poverty level. If you made enough money this week to keep your family from homelessness and starvation, I'm satisfied for you." Not the standard? I didn't think so.

If your electronic gradebook system allows, set your notifications to alert you each time a teacher enters a score of zero. If not, you check, frequently. Chances are very good that if each zero is addressed swiftly and ruthlessly, the issue of failing will never be an issue at all. In addition,

Successfully Navigating High School
A Guide for Students Entering High School and Their Parents, Because
the Path to Graduating with Honors Begins in Ninth Grade

if a child takes a class and doesn't make as high a grade on his report card as his or her parent might like, but that child has not earned zeroes, chances are good that the child is giving his best or at least a good effort. As a parent, that has to be enough.

Don't check the electronic grade book every day. Many times the teacher only updates once a week or so. Checking the grade book every day will frustrate both parent and child. Have the grade book notify you once, at most twice a week and, as I said, for zeroes. You check, too, but again, no more than once or twice a week.

I've heard may parents say, "My child is in high school now. It's time for me to step back." Parents, this is not the time to take off the training wheels and allow the child to take care of his or her own business. There is too much at stake. There is too much to lose. You'll have time to take off the training wheels, to stop making certain he or she is making good decisions after graduation.

I think about the famous incident from the Barcelona Olympics. Derek Richardson, favored to be a gold medalist, pulled a muscle in a race he'd run thousands of times. But rather than allow himself to be carried from the track on a stretcher, he insisted on finishing the race he'd traveled thousands of miles and spent thousands of hours in preparation to run. In pain and tears he struggled to limp to the finish line, when a man broke through the crowd, "That's my son." With his dad's help, Derek hobbled to the finish line. His Dad released Derek so that he could finish his race, then get the medical attention he needed.

Derek Richardson did not win that race. He's done everything right. His choices had all been the best of choices. He was where he was supposed to be, having worked hard to get there. And yet, ultimately, he needed the support of a loving parent. Your student does too.

A final thought about the electronic grade book; many times grades, especially a drastic change in grades is one of the first indications that something else is going wrong in a teenager's life. Maybe he or she is making poor choices in terms of his or her friends or drug or alcohol use. A child who becomes sexually active and begins to smoke marijuana often forgets to study for his Physics test. Then oops his grade plummets. The parent sees, right away that there is a problem and has a spring board from which to ask questions. Grades should not be the entire focus of school, but they should certainly be an important focus.

Successfully Navigating High School
A Guide for Students Entering High School and Their Parents, Because
the Path to Graduating with Honors Begins in Ninth Grade

E MAIL

Picture this. You're busy. You're cooking the evening meal, keeping your children from killing one another, watching the news to make certain your company has not imploded destroying your hopes for retirement, when, wouldn't you know it, the phone rings, and who is it? Well what does he want? It's your child's teacher. Calling you. Wanting to talk. A long time. By the time you get off the phone, it's too late to cook. You're going to have to go get fast food and your family will have to die a slow death from salt and fat. Don't get angry at the teacher. It's your fault. My fault? Yes. Your fault. Here's what I think you should do so that this never happens again.

During the first week of school, for each of your children, e mail each teacher. Lie. Say that you are looking forward to this year. Tell the teacher that you have heard of his or her wonderful class and are looking forward to blah, blah, blah.

Here's a sample:

Dear Mrs. Teachmealot,

I hope you had a restful summer and are as excited about this coming school year as I am. My son, John, is in your third period class. He was thrilled as he shared with me all the exciting topics you will study this year. John's Dad, Fred and I want you to know that we have set high standards for John and are vitally interested in John's education. Please don't hesitate to contact us should you

13

need our support.

Thank you for this opportunity to partner with you in John's education.

Sincerely,
John's Mom

Ok. You tell me. If you're John's teacher do you delete this e mail with a "Yea, right!" or do you save this e mail and at the first sign of trouble with John, you go back into it, hit the return key and contact this concerned parent? That's what's called a rhetorical question, because the answer is too obvious for it to be just a regular question. If you set up lines of communication, the teacher is going to use the lines you initiate. You just made it easy for the teacher to contact you. In addition, your son, John, has been culled from the pack. The teacher knows that if he or she doesn't contact you, there will be questions asked, for example, "why not?" If you don't open these lines, the teacher will only call you if the problem is a critical one. Do you want John's teacher to wait until John is failing before she says to herself, "Well, I guess I had better call John's parents so they can start saving for summer school."

And then there's the side benefit; you can stay out of fast food restaurants because you'll be able to cook supper, uninterrupted, and read your e mail after the kids have gone to bed.

Successfully Navigating High School
A Guide for Students Entering High School and Their Parents, Because
the Path to Graduating with Honors Begins in Ninth Grade

THE DANGERS OF SOCIAL MEDIA

Students, I know you don't believe me. No one ever does, but one day, someone you don't know will make a decision that alters the course of your life based on what he or she sees on your social media. You must think of your social media as a protracted job interview.

Stop for a minute. Go to one of your social media pages. Go through your history. Now imagine you are going through the pages with your potential employer over one shoulder and the dean of admissions to the University of your Choice over the other shoulder. A little uncomfortable?

Anything you put on social media does not belong to you anymore. The social media sites sell your page contents to schools and large employers. If the job you're after involves a deep fryer or a cash register, you won't have to worry about your potential employer one day checking your social media site. If the job you desire involves a suit and tie or hose, name plates instead of name badges, an office or cubicle instead of a cash register, then you will have to worry about social media. It's a fact of life.

Don't believe me? Some things are true whether you believe them or not.

CHAPTER 2
FRESHMAN YEAR
WHAT EVERY PARENT OF A FRESHMAN AND EVERY FRESHMAN STUDENT SHOULD KNOW GOING INTO HIS OR HER FRESHMAN YEAR.

Successfully Navigating High School
A Guide for Students Entering High School and Their Parents, Because
the Path to Graduating with Honors Begins in Ninth Grade

Having Our Materials

First grade was quite a shock to me. I learned quite a bit in first grade and most of what I learned wasn't necessarily in the curriculum. (I'll leave what I learned about race relations and the social and sexual dynamic of first grade to another time and place more appropriate.) One thing I learned very quickly was the social dynamic surrounding the borrowing of supplies. To say I was a spoiled child is to call a trans-Atlantic flight, "crossing the pond." I would go to the store with my Papa or my parents and I would see bright, shiny supplies that would surely cause me to be a Rhodes Scholar, and my parents would procure them for me. My parents were working class people, but it was unusual for them not to get for me items that could make my school work more palatable. I swiftly learned, however, that I must also keep, at all times, cheap, yet reliable, supplies for the borrowers. There were some in my class, who never, never had their own supplies. The teacher would instruct the class to get out a sheet of paper and a pencil. One would think this to be a relatively simple request, but alas, no. Such a request was always, always followed by a chorus of, "I need a pencil. I need some paper." I soon learned that if you loan one pencil that is OK, but that one sheet of paper is unacceptable. The borrower would complain that he or she needed multiple sheets in order to have an acceptable writing surface. Even at six years old, I was bothered that the individual did not provide his own acceptable writing surface. I learned that the social price of saying this to the individual was too high and that my parents did not complain when I requested more paper. Perhaps they thought I was doing much more work than I really was.

As a classroom teacher, I see the same dynamics are still in place. When, as a teacher, I request that the students get out a pen and a sheet of paper (shocking given the setting – a high school class room), I often hear the murmurs of borrowing.

It doesn't bother me anymore. It just is. But I have continued to take mental notes. I know who will have trouble in my class. I know whose parents I will have to call and call and call.

Let's just be very honest and straightforward here. If you haven't made certain you have some paper and a pen or pencil before you come to school, perhaps schoolwork is not going to be your priority today.

Parent, you can make the difference here. You can make this, if not your child's priority, at least an item on his radar. Ask the question, "Do you have paper and something to write with?" A spiral notebook and a pencil together cost less than the price of a soda. By asking this question, by letting your child know that his or her supplies are your priority, you've put your child on notice, "I expect you to do some work today."

When I was in first grade, I had a classmate named Michael. That really was his name. I could make one up, but really, why? You don't know him. He never had his supplies. Never. No paper. No pencil. No crayons. No map pencils. Just a vast desert of nothing.

One evening we had PTA Open House. Parents came to school. They looked in our classrooms at our desks. They talked to the teacher. They saw our work. My parents came. They even brought my little brother. I was so proud for them to see my environment. I was most curious, however, when I saw that Michael's parents had come, his mom and his step-dad. I really was surprised that he had parents. It's now over forty years later, but I remember as clearly as I remember this morning, looking

Successfully Navigating High School
A Guide for Students Entering High School and Their Parents, Because
the Path to Graduating with Honors Begins in Ninth Grade

over to see silent tears streaming down Michael's Mom's face at the sight of his empty supply box and non-existent work, then his step-dad, in his work books and dirty Dickie's shirt, squat down until he was eye-to-eye with Michael as he said, "Son, when you need something, you need to tell us and we will get it for you."

I can guess now what I couldn't at six that Michael was reluctant to request supplies, or anything probably, as he adjusted to his place in a blended family.

Michael's lack of supplies was reflective of a deeper problem. He didn't bring paper and pencils with him to school because he didn't intend to do any work that day. He had more serious issues to worry about.

After that day, although my memory becomes hazy here, having issues of my own, Michael no longer needed my supplies. There were others, but not Michael. What do I remember? He and I went through school together. We graduated together. Somewhere along the line, school became a priority for Michael. I have to believe, that big man, squatting down to the little boy and looking him eye-to-eye and telling him that he would have what he needed, made a big difference. Does your child have what he or she needs? Do you know? Have you asked? Does your child know that this is a priority for you? Maybe he or she should?

What do I think a high school student needs? I say forget those big binders. I think a student needs one folder or small binder for notebook paper, a pocket folder for each class to keep returned, graded work, a homework folder, along with an assignment book. You need a pen and pencil, more than one; they break. Keep your graded papers separate, but your homework and due dates in one place. Review your homework folder, your due dates and your calendar every day. Work on things as you go, don't wait until the day before something is due before you work on it.

Part of your homework each night is to take a mental inventory of what you will do in class, each class, the next day. If you have been paying attention, you will know. If you don't know, then you have some questions to ask yourself. A student should go to school knowing, at least approximately what he will be doing in each class on any given day, at least generally. Your teachers tell you. Review it in your mind. Go into Algebra class, thinking about what you did yesterday and what you will probably do today. Get your homework out on your desk. Go to school with the express purpose of doing your best. I like that word, purpose. Whether you're a high school freshman or a forty year old working guy or gal, it is readily apparent to all, those who sleep-walk through life and those who live on purpose. That is not my original concept, I know. Shades of this concept go back to Greek philosophy and still further back to Solomon. It's still true now.

Successfully Navigating High School
A Guide for Students Entering High School and Their Parents, Because
the Path to Graduating with Honors Begins in Ninth Grade

The GPA

Ask any student who is currently in the top ten percent of his or her class, "What is the most important year for your GPA?" (That's grade point average, the single most important number of your high school career.) The GPA is the one number that can tell the onlooker how hard you worked and how successful you were in your efforts. Unless that student's high school has a GPA calculation method different from any other I have ever seen, or heard of, the answer to that question is "freshman year." It's simple math. The fewer numbers, the more easily effected the average. The more numbers involved, the more difficult it is to move the average up. (Moving it down seems to be easy, no matter what.)

One of my former students, Katelyn Holliness, now a graduate of the University of North Texas, had this to say about her freshman year, "My freshman year I was a perfectionist, but not in the good way. If I felt like my work wasn't good enough, I would stress myself out and sometimes turn my work in late, which stressed me out even more. It damaged my performance and potential to have a higher GPA, which I deeply regretted."

Katelyn went on the say, "Striving for excellence, and timeliness in high school is the perfect way to get into the college you want and to gain experience and train yourself for what's ahead."

Great advice, Katelyn.

Another one of my former students, Katie Morrow, a

graduate of the University of Texas at Dallas, says, "Freshman year was a HUGE culture shock! I still can't get over the fact that the only two C's that I have ever received were Freshman year. (one in science, one in math.) I dropped out of Pre-AP math because of it! And I was bored to tears in regulars' classes...

Most of my struggles in high school I think stem from not having a lot of parental support ESPECIALLY for freshman year. I think it is ok for parents to hover a little the first year of high school just until a kid finds his footing. I think it is the only year the parents can probably still get away with a little hand holding...

I think it was hard for my parents to help me because neither one of my parents has a background in academia. They are both blue collar workers. I think they thought they weren't up to par in their knowledge enough to help me adapt to high school. Looking back I think even if they were involved through encouraging me to participate in extracurricular activities it would've helped me feel more confident...I always felt like a burden on them with after school activities, and I didn't sign up for them until I could drive myself. Once I was able to be truly involved in the school, I truly started to bloom."

Wow, Katie, your advice is profound. I'll bet that if Katie had told her parents what she was feeling, things might have been different for her. Clearly Katie's parents loved her, love her still and wanted only what is best for her, just like you do for your child.

Katie is a success story. She did become involved. She did take mostly advanced classes. She did finish college. She does have her degree. You can't see me, but right now, I'm standing and shouting for Katie.

Successfully Navigating High School
A Guide for Students Entering High School and Their Parents, Because
the Path to Graduating with Honors Begins in Ninth Grade

If a student completes a successful freshman year, everything is simpler. If freshman year was a disaster, you can mitigate the damage, but, again, like everything else in life, it's easier to do it correctly the first time, and although damage can be mitigated, it cannot be totally erased.

I love the Chinese Proverb, "The best time to plant a tree is twenty years ago. The second best time is today." This is your life. You can't just give up and go cry in the corner. Disastrous freshman year? That's too bad; buckle down now. Start today.

If you are lucky enough to be reading this page when your child is still in elementary school, please listen. Grades in elementary school and most of middle school do not follow your child. What is most important is that he or she learn as much as possible. Duh? Right? Well, no, based on my observations, parents will often shift their students/children down, into less challenging classes until they reach the point where the child is comfortable and making good grades. Grades don't matter in elementary school, even for the most part in middle school. Put your child in the most challenging class your school guidance counselor will allow you. Don't accept a no. If your child is not failing, he or she is learning. If your child is uncomfortable, he or she is really learning. If your child is making perfect scores and is experiencing no dissidence, he or she is learning nothing. That's not acceptable; that's irresponsible.

Teach your child to learn as much as he can, as early as he can, because in high school, it WILL matter. In high school advanced placement and dual credit classes get higher grade points, and they should. If you're going to take the harder class later, you will need the foundation. Go for the higher class. Go for the tougher teacher. In the words of Jim Rohn, "The Pain of Discipline or the Pain of Regret and Disappointment." You don't get to the top of the mountain from the bunny slope. (That one is mine.) Get off the bunny slope. How does the analogy translate? It translates into every assignment, every day. I will turn in every assignment, every day. I will do my best on every assignment, every day. I will purpose to learn all I can, every, every, every day.

Your GPA begins in high school, sometimes in a select few middle school classes. Start today. Build your GPA. Don't obsess and worry; work, learn.

I did a little arithmetic one day and determined that over the course of my career, I've taught almost five thousand teenagers. Presently, I work in a high school of approximately 3000 students. Before this one, I worked in a high school of approximately 2000 students. My first high school had a population of approximately 2500 students. At different times in my career, I have taught all on-level classes. At others I've taught all advanced placement classes. Mostly, like most teachers, I've taught a mixture. I have taught many wonderful students whom I will remember all of my life. I have taught students who got their college degrees. I've taught students who went on to become teachers and policemen. (Yes, one of them gave me a ticket for running a red light. I was so proud.) I've taught students who went to trade school who went on to be mechanics and morticians. I have also taught students who have gone on to die in prison. (...not so proud about that...)

From my limited experience, what I've observed is that the best thing a student can do for his or her GPA is stick with advanced placement and dual credit classes. I've known students who were in the top ten percent of their class who took mostly on-level classes, but they're rare.

In today's competitive market place, students in the top ten percent of their class are getting turned away from the colleges and universities of their choice. If you want your choice, you may have to be in the top five to seven percent

Successfully Navigating High School
A Guide for Students Entering High School and Their Parents, Because
the Path to Graduating with Honors Begins in Ninth Grade

of your class.

For almost two decades now, across two school districts, I've taught over two dozen valedictorians and salutatorians.

So what?

They talk and I listen. Every year I ask them about their study habits. And what they say is very similar; it sounds like this. I didn't start out to be the valedictorian. I started out to do my best. I was surprised when the class ranking results came out and I was number one. But once I saw that I was, I was determined to maintain my placement.

That's right. If you are to be a high ranking senior, you must, must, must be a high ranking lower classman.

My valedictorians tell me the same tale, consistently, they say, I just did my best, every day. I did my assignment even when I didn't want to. Even when I didn't see the sense in the assignment, I trusted that my teacher had some reason for giving it to me. I completed the assignments given to me, even if I knew there would be no grade, but sometimes, just to learn something. I listened and I worked.

Some Valedictorians are painfully smart, but in my experience, admittedly limited, the painfully smart kids are often number three or four. The Valedictorian is the determined one. The worker. The "show me an obstacle so I can climb it" one. Admittedly, also very intelligent, but often more balanced. They have their eye on the goal, but very often that goal is not the Valedictorian's medal. Often that goal is to do their best every day, on every assignment.

(As an aside, think of what Adults could accomplish if we completed every task well, if we gave our best effort, every time. The possibilities boggle the mind.)

If you wait until your senior year to try to improve your GPA to the point that it looks acceptable to the University of your choice, you will probably be one of those experiencing Rohn's "pain of regret and disappointment."

Listen to the advice of Jehadu Abshiro, one of my former students, now a graduate of Southern Methodist University, employed at a successful local business.

"Looking back, I would urge high school students to take core classes seriously. As someone studying and working in the media, a fair amount of content that I was sure I would never use past high school reappears in my work constantly. Whether it's combing through financial documents and using formulas from calculus or referencing a line from a Romantic poem, having that information mentally handy makes my work much easier. I learned early on that the information I learned in high school is the foundation of a college education. Memorizing books isn't necessary, but developing connections between the information you learn in science, math, history and English is essential in the vast majority of majors and careers. I wish I had put in more effort, time and energy in those four subjects."

As Jehadu's teacher, I can assure you she put in much effort, but that's the thing about highly successful people, they pinpoint what they need to know. They target it and they go about gaining what they need in a purposeful manner.

Successfully Navigating High School
A Guide for Students Entering High School and Their Parents, Because
the Path to Graduating with Honors Begins in Ninth Grade

THE CLASSES YOU TAKE WILL MAKE A DIFFERENCE

Parents, encourage your child to take the tough class. Ask for the toughest teacher. Pain now or pain later? When they get tired, walk them by the aisle in Walmart where they sell hairnets. Take a walk by the deli and feel the heat from the deep-fryer. I once heard a parent say that sleeping is for the grave and for people who aspire to have careers that involve hair nets, name tags, and phrases like, "Would you like fries with that?" When your child is up later than you'd like, doing homework, while the neighbor's children are lulled to sleep by their video games, think about the direct correlation between level of education and future earnings. It's not all about money you say? I couldn't agree more. The further your child goes in his or her education, and that doesn't always mean college, the more choice he or she will have, the more content he or she will be in his or her chosen field, and bottom line, the happier he or she will be in the whole of his or her life. Be strong for your children. They won't always make the hard choice without your guidance, and once they are old enough and wise enough to make a better choice, the window of opportunity may have passed.

Do I really have to decide that now? Yes. Yes you do. If your child were my child, I would start my child in all Pre-AP classes. Your counselor will try to tell you that the load is too heavy, that your child cannot take it. What they ought to tell you is that if it's just really too much, the schedule can be changed, but that starting off your high school career in the on-level course practically assures finishing your high school career in the on-level course.

Giving your child a possibility to fail also means giving him a chance to succeed.

But I'm a teacher. What do students say? Here is what one of my former students, Stephanie Taylor has to say. Stephanie was the Valedictorian of her graduating class and four years later a graduate with honors of Texas Christian University. After working as a RN, she is now going on to Medical School. She says, "Too many high school students make the excuse that they 'don't care' about the subjects presented in high school because some of the topics may not be directly pertinent to their future careers. I've heard this as an excuse for either not putting in effort or not taking upper level AP/IB classes. Some students say, 'I will start studying harder when I get to college.' You cannot train for a marathon overnight and you should not expect to train for college overnight either. Getting involved in AP/IB classes and in extracurricular activities mentally trains a student for the long hours of focused study that are required in college.

College is not just difficult for the workload, but for the curveballs life throws you when you are 18 to 22 years old. You are away from home for the first time, no one reminds you to do your homework, and there are distractions everywhere. In my college career, I battled a six-month case of mononucleosis, participated on the dance team, worked as a Resident Assistant in the dorms, and had surgery requiring a lengthy recovery. Despite the distractions and the setbacks, I graduated college in four years because I maintained focus and continued the study techniques I learned in high school. Practice and train now by taking upper level AP/IB courses so that when life throws you those curveballs, you already have the academic habits that will allow you to persevere and to graduate on time.

I've heard from my brother and from other smart kids who refuse to apply themselves fully in high school. 'These classes don't help me' or 'I'll never use this.' They think

Successfully Navigating High School
A Guide for Students Entering High School and Their Parents, Because
the Path to Graduating with Honors Begins in Ninth Grade

because they barely tried and made A's and B's throughout high school that they will breeze through college. The A's and B's give them a false sense of security. They try to avoid AP Chemistry, AP Anatomy and Physiology, AP Biology, AP English Literature, and BC Calculus because it would require more effort, when those are the only classes that truly force a student to study and to get organized. They don't take into account that at 18 they have to learn to study and to live away from home at the same time."

Stephanie has her Bachelors of Nursing Science Degree and is a registered nurse, practicing at a local hospital in Texas before deciding to continue to Medical School. Did that just happen? No it is the result of a series of good decisions. Where will you be four years after you graduate from high school? Will you still be wondering what you want to do with your life or will you be living it, like Stephanie?

Parents, as an aside, if your child is still bewildered and undecided about his or her future four or five years after graduation, he or she is probably going to be bewildered and undecided in your house. It is in your best interests to help your child to find a purposeful, meaningful path, one that leads to success, one that leads out of your house.

You don't want to listen to Stephanie? Maybe you'll listen to Sarah.

Hi! I'm Sarah Mirza, a graduate of [removed] High School's Class of 2008 and a proud alumnus of Mrs. Baxter's AP English Language and Literature courses. I went on to New York University from little ole [removed], Texas, where I received my Bachelor of Arts in Politics and History with Latin Honors and I then received my Masters in Public Administration in International Policy and Management from NYU Wagner Graduate School of Public Service. In my six years since graduating high school, my pursuit of higher education came along with great opportunities as well: I traveled to 30 countries, lived and studied in London and Abu Dhabi for some time, and interned at various United Nations agencies for three years in a row.

I may sound like I have it together, but believe me, it was a difficult journey full of insecurity and confusion at times. As the only child of Pakistani immigrants, it was hard knowing the right place to kick off my academic journey, as well as the kinds of resources and tools I should have been taking advantage of in high school. Luckily, that's where wonderful teachers like Mrs. Baxter came in to help guide me and give me the reassurance I needed to achieve my dreams and move to the Big Apple!

At [removed] High School, the majority of us were introduced to AP classes during our junior year, and, for most of us, our first AP class was the dreaded English Language with Mrs. Baxter. Up until Junior year, English and writing-based classes were all fun and games—read a few classic novels, dissected a few poems, gave a few presentations. But, Mrs. Baxter's AP classes were no joke. Mrs. Baxter had a reputation for being a hard grader and really challenging her students throughout their junior and senior years.

I still remember the anxiety I felt on days we had to do timed writings in preparation for the AP test, and the more severe anxiety on days we were getting our grades back. These English classes were tough, yes, but truly the most important classes I took in high school. No classes could have prepared me better for college, and while I recognized how effective my writing was becoming, I didn't truly value my new, honed skill until my freshman year at NYU. Mrs. Baxter trained us well, gave us well-

Successfully Navigating High School
A Guide for Students Entering High School and Their Parents, Because
the Path to Graduating with Honors Begins in Ninth Grade

established guidelines, and always gave us direct feedback in justification of why we got the grade we did—these are all luxuries that are not very well utilized by college professors. What Mrs. Baxter did, if taken seriously by students, was provide a framework for improvement and motivation for the places where our analysis, critique, or style was on point. If you have a teacher now who disappointingly does not always adhere to providing consistent and constant feedback on your writing, I highly suggest sitting down with your teacher and asking for thorough comments.

Your high school English/writing classes, especially the one you take senior year, will be your foundation for college. Your freshman year of college you may be enrolled in a Foundations of Writing or Writing 101 sort of class, but, believe me, those, while framed as introductory courses, don't at all come with the expectations of introductory courses. By the time you get to college your professors will fully expect you to be able to write a well-crafted, thoughtful, thought-provoking, and critical essay with no grammatical errors.

Listen, I know high school doesn't always give us the most necessary tools we need to succeed in college, and sometimes it doesn't even fully prepare us for college-level courses no matter how many APs we take. As someone who has always been interested in international politics and who went to a high school that had a limited offering in the politics realm, it was always a bit difficult (especially junior and senior year) to really devote myself to classes that I felt weren't furthering the pursuit of my goals. I knew I had to take these classes and I had to do well in them to be a competitive college applicant, but I understand that it's hard to be invested in something when you know not much of it will help you once you're actually in college. But, the one exception to this (ok, there's probably a few others) is definitely taking a challenging English class.

Work on your writing style and quality when you're in high school and have your own style by the time you leave high school. Whatever your major will be in college, whatever kind of coursework you take, there will always be a writing component where the value of having a concise way to deliver your message through words on paper will never be undermined. High school is your time to invest in this asset and it's something you will have forever. Even when it comes to jobs and internships, I have never been on an interview where I wasn't asked to provide a writing sample or strong written communication wasn't a requirement.

Now, I know not every academic journey and career path is as writing-intensive as others, however, the skills that you gain from being a strong writer are insurmountable. In college, I never had a class I didn't have to write at least one essay for, including cell biology and statistics. The ability to write well is the ability to be creative, analytical, perceptive to other sides and arguments, as well as bolstering your own argument with research and evidence. These are not just skills required in all fields and throughout life, but are transferrable skills you can always apply to different areas. The care and precision it takes to craft an argument with no holes is the same as what a mathematician needs to be able to look through an algorithm or calculation to make sure there are no errors. The use of proof and evidence is just as vital to writing an effective paper on Shakespearean era literature as it is to a doctor when a medical discovery is made or to a politician when trying to advance a policy. And, the ability to write thoughtfully about all sides of an issue can easily be transferred to when you're traveling the world to far and exotic places and are trying to understand and be open to cultural differences. So, take your writing classes seriously in high school even if you're not crazy about the

Successfully Navigating High School
A Guide for Students Entering High School and Their Parents, Because
the Path to Graduating with Honors Begins in Ninth Grade

content and work on your writing quality. Take your teacher's help in nurturing your ability and fostering your style so you have one less thing to worry about when you get to college!

Wow, Sarah, thank you. I did not pay her to say that. I didn't tell her what to say. Sarah is far beyond me now. She says what she wants. She does what she wants because she worked hard during high school and college. She made good decisions at a crucial point and it has made the difference for her.

Yet however compelling and persuasive Stephanie and Sarah may be, the most convincing argument I've ever heard, came from my student, Deesha Patel, who stated, "All throughout middle school, I was in regulars classes. I always thought that only the highly gifted intellectuals could handle it. My teachers made it sound so much harder than it really was which scared me out of taking those classes. My seventh grade math teacher encouraged me to take honors classes in high school and that changed my high school experience. She saw the potential I had to succeed in advanced placement classes, and she encouraged me to take two math classes my sophomore year to catch up to the rest of my class. I realized the vast differences between Pre-AP classes and regulars classes pretty fast. I never had to study before, and it was all so overwhelming. It was completely feasible, but a hard change to make. I wish that I had taken honors classes in middle school to prepare me for the classes I took in high school. I have seen how much more in-depth honors classes go, and I am very glad that I decided to take AP classes in high school. I have been placed in a better learning environment, and am able to say that I have received an exceptional education from my AP teachers.

These teachers truly care about the students and will look out for their best interests. It was their motivation and encouraging words that kept me going in high school. I would encourage incoming freshman to try to take as many honors classes as you can. I know that these classes will help tremendously when they go to college, and it will overall prepare them for better futures. I ended up being in the top ten students at my high school, which I could not have been without taking more challenging classes."

Deesha, your story is one for the ages, a student who challenged herself and ended up on the stage with the top ten. That is an American success story!

Successfully Navigating High School
A Guide for Students Entering High School and Their Parents, Because
the Path to Graduating with Honors Begins in Ninth Grade

The Resume

Freshman year is really not too early to begin writing your resume, to start compiling a list of what you're going to put on your resume. The educational resume is more important than you think. It's a love letter to your college or university. It's more of an essay than the college essay. It says, "I will finish my degree and not hurt your ratings. I work hard." List your AP or Dual Credit classes on your educational resume, if the list is impressive. If the list is pitifully short, leave it off. Your Senior year is too late to compile an impressive list. You will have great difficulty taking the tough Senior level AP courses that will make your resume shine if you did not take the tough Pre-AP classes as a freshman and a sophomore.

Your resume will be a reflection of your decision to take the tougher path. As freshmen this is hard to see, but when in the fall of the senior year, seniors start finalizing their resumes, the truth is stark and sometimes ugly.

Ok, we are taking the tough classes. That's got to be enough, right? Not even close. You must be deeply involved in student life organizations. Colleges and Universities want students who will make quality alumni. Involved high school students make involved college students, and then quality alumni.

Divide your opportunities into categories: school, community, church. Do some volunteer work in each of these areas each semester. Are you in the band? I would be extraordinarily surprised if the band does not involve itself in a volunteer experience each school year. It doesn't?

Look for one. Many non-profit organizations are looking for free labor. They need you and you need them. But it doesn't need to be that hard. Help your student council with its food drive. Help your class decorate for homecoming. Volunteer with toy distributing efforts at Christmas time. My high school has an organization that makes mums for special needs children for homecoming. Your high school has something too. I guarantee you it does. Start your freshman year building your resume and don't stop. Your educational resume will transition into your career resume. Its importance cannot be overstated.

Successfully Navigating High School
A Guide for Students Entering High School and Their Parents, Because
the Path to Graduating with Honors Begins in Ninth Grade

THE PSAT

The spring of your freshman year is the time to start thinking about the PSAT. Put a SAT question of the day app on your phone. Complete free practice tests from your school library website. Chant PSAT as you dress each morning. It's more important than you think.

Why are we not talking more about the PSAT? You take the PSAT as a Sophomore, and then again as a Junior to compete for National Merit. As a Sophomore, you're probably thinking more about the homecoming dance than about how you're going to pay for college, but for pure bang for the buck, the PSAT is the one.

Don't go into the PSAT without study, especially if you are generally a strong student. The PSAT is the one that can make all the difference for you. It can bring people to your door who you want to talk to. National Merit Scholars are determined by the PSAT. (The one you take your Junior Year) National Merit Scholarships are the Papa Bears of awards available to high school students. I challenge you to research advantages available to National Merit Scholars, then tell me a little study for the test is not worthwhile.

And what do most of us do? We go in cold. We take the PSAT because it's good practice for the SAT, which it is, with no inkling of the difference it could make if we did well.

If you are the parent of a freshman, think PSAT. Think practice. If your child says to you, "Mom, Dad I'm sure I'll do fine," think of that time when you thought, "I know the warning light is on, but I'm sure I don't need to go to the gas station, this very minute." Parent, this is the time. Now. Be strong. Be persistent. I have a mental image for you that I think will help. Ready? Picture that surly 14-year-old who lives in your house still living there when he or she is 24, maybe 34. I thought that would do it. Think PSAT. Let's say it together P-S-A-T. Very good.

Successfully Navigating High School
A Guide for Students Entering High School and Their Parents, Because
the Path to Graduating with Honors Begins in Ninth Grade

ACADEMIC DISHONESTY

As an educator, this is one topic that bothers me, but as a Mom, I just don't understand it. When my son was very young, he played soccer, sort of. He ran on the field with the other boys. He kicked the ball and occasionally it would go in the general direction he expected it to go. He understood the concept. Kick the ball down the field and finally into the net. He initially missed one very important concept though. The concept? It's very important to kick the ball into the correct net. If you kick the ball into the wrong net, you make points for the other team. We don't hate the other team. Some of the people on the other team are people we go to church and school with. We like them. They're our friends, but they need to make their own points. I advise you to say this to people who want to 'borrow' your homework. I know you're my friend and I really like you, but you're going to have to do your own homework. We're in a contest, and the winner gets to sit closer to the front of the auditorium at graduation. The winner is more likely to get to go to the college or university of his choice. The winner is more likely to get grants and scholarships to help to pay for college. I like you, but why would I help you to win? I want to win. I especially want to beat you. It's not personal, but winning is better.

In the bigger picture, academic dishonesty will get you expelled in college. It will get you fired in the work place....and it should. What do I have that's more important than my intellectual property? Steal my car, but don't steal my ideas. Don't steal the product of my brain, the result of all I know and have experienced. Someone who would steal intellectual property, would steal anything. This is not someone you can trust. This is not someone you want in your life. This is not your friend.

My very favorite story about the theft of ideas is taken from an incident involving the absolutely gifted writer, Leonard Pitts, Jr. whose work was taken and published by another who represented it as his own. Leonard Pitts, Jr. said it best, "Get your own damn words. Leave mine alone."

Successfully Navigating High School
A Guide for Students Entering High School and Their Parents, Because
the Path to Graduating with Honors Begins in Ninth Grade

STUDENT LIFE

Be involved in something. Band, drill team, choir, theater, athletics are always great choices, but what if you don't have the money, the talent, the skill? Then join student council. They need people who will work hard. You can do that. Volunteer with your Class. They need you. Whatever your skill, there is a high school organization for you. Talk to your counselor. Talk to your teacher, any teacher. Teachers get up every morning hoping today will be the day they get to really make a difference for someone. Let it be you. Go to your teacher. Tell him or her that you really think you will be a more successful student if you are more involved in student life. I guarantee you that after he or she has picked his or her chin off the ground, he or she will help you. If, unfortunately, you have one of the few teachers who has lost his way, wait until the next class and try again. School is by design full of paths to involve you. Students who are more involved are almost without exception more successful.

In the words of one of my former students, Dani Glenn, a highly successful student in high school and currently a graduate of the University of Arkansas, "As cheesy as it may be, you only live once is especially true in regards to high school. You have one chance to be in as many social activities as possible. One chance to learn the basics that help you to succeed in college. And one chance to find good friends and make relationships that last a lifetime. Study hard, thank your teachers every chance you get, and enjoy the time you have with your friends and family. It'll be over before you know it! College is great, but only if you really lived in high school, academically and socially."

Thank you, Dani. That's stellar advice for anyone, freshman or not.

Go to dances. There is almost always a homecoming dance. You'll have more fun if you go with a group of friends, same sex friends. Leave the romance for later. It just complicates things, but that's another topic. Dance at the dance. Talk. Laugh.

Go to the football games and other sporting events. Of course if you're part of the band or drill team, that is a foregone conclusion, but if you're not, still, go to the games. Go with friends. Be a part of student life. Being a part of student life on Friday night will make you a better student on Monday morning.

Successfully Navigating High School
A Guide for Students Entering High School and Their Parents, Because
the Path to Graduating with Honors Begins in Ninth Grade

WHAT SENIORS SAY THEY WISH THEY HAD KNOWN AS FRESHMEN

I asked my seniors a question, "If your spring -of-your-senior-year self could tell your fall-of-your-freshman-year self anything, what would it be?

I wanted a spontaneous response, not a studied one, so I gave them only about 4 minutes to answer and I limited their responses to one sentence. Here is what I got, uncensored and raw:

- "Don't be so shy, and instead be more open to making new friends."
- "Spend more time studying for the SAT and ACT."
- "Don't slack off."
- "Spend more time getting to know people."
- "No matter how much you don't think it matters whether or not the homework gets done, you should always do what the teacher assigns."
- "Be confident in everything you do."
- "Focus on your schooling. You get paid for knowledge."
- "GPA counts."
- "Keep up with your work."
- "Your Junior year is your most important year because ACT and SAT are important ."

- "Senioritis is real."
- "I wish I'd know who I was as a person before now."
- "GPA does actually count."
- "It's Ok to talk to others and speak your mind."
- "Be responsible in everything you do."
- "I wish I'd learned to really study earlier."
- "Apply for housing early!"
- "Choose your friends carefully."
- "Be yourself. Don't change for anyone."
- "Freshman year is the most important year."
- "Join more clubs."
- "Dual Credit classes do not require an expensive test."
- "Time really does go by fast."
- "You reap what you sow."
- "People's emotions and relationships are tricky."
- "AP Classes are stressful."
- "Don't be late."
- "There is no excuse for missing school."
- "Don't let things bother you."
- "I don't have to have it together all the time."
- "Eliminate negative people from your life."
- "There is not enough time for everything."
- "Focus on the future and don't worry so much about the present."
- "Don't sweat the small things. Focus on friends, fun, and working hard."
- "Follow your dreams; ignore what people say, because when you're at the top they won't matter a bit."
- "Don't allow anyone to tell you that you can't do something."
- "Work hard; persistence is key and thank God

Successfully Navigating High School
A Guide for Students Entering High School and Their Parents, Because
the Path to Graduating with Honors Begins in Ninth Grade

when it's all said and done."

- "Take chances. Make mistakes. Learn from them."
- "Don't procrastinate."
- "Don't waste your time worrying about other people's opinions. "
- "Taking regular classes will kill your GPA."
- "Prepare yourself to succeed even when everything goes wrong."
- "It gets better."
- "Enjoy the time you spend in high school; it goes very fast."
- "Try my best in everything I do."
- "Live for yourself, not others."
- "Balance study, work, and social life."
- "Don't worry about what other people think of me."
- "Take advantage of every moment and live life to the fullest."
- "Don't wish for your senior year. Spend every moment enjoying where you are. "
- "Work hard."
- "Focus on schoolwork and friendships instead of stressing over a relationship."
- "Homework is important, especially in subjects related to math."
- "Don't wait around for something to happen."
- "Don't think you don't need anyone."
- "Have more fun. Don't be so serious."
- "Be more independent."
- "Don't worry about a singular 'big' test because it will all work out okay in the end."
- "Hard work pays off and things happen as they

should."
- "Don't be afraid or ashamed to ask for help."
- "It's better to work hard in the beginning, before you get tired."

Successfully Navigating High School
A Guide for Students Entering High School and Their Parents, Because
the Path to Graduating with Honors Begins in Ninth Grade

ADVICE FROM MY DAUGHTER, FINLEA BAXTER TO HIGH SCHOOL FRESHMEN, WRITTEN WHEN SHE WAS A FRESHMAN AT THE UNIVERSITY OF OKLAHOMA

Don't throw away your freshman year. It'll come back to bite you in the hind-parts.

Listen to what your teachers are telling you about your future, but listen to what God is telling you, too. And don't shortchange your instincts; if a path feels like it's not for you, do not follow it, no matter what the adults around you say. Honestly, they're as lost and confused as you are. They just happen to be better at hiding it.

Don't listen to over-the-top people. What I mean is that, yes, you should ignore the horrible things people say, but you should also be careful about believing your own press. You're going to do great things, but let's face it; you're not a child marvel. Everyone has room for improvement. Take encouragement, but remain humble.

Boys: Remember to give the females around you the respect they're due.

Girls: Be deserving of that respect

In all likelihood, this romantic relationship you're in

won't last past next week. Yes, you love him/her more than life itself, yada yada yada. But the statistical likelihood of this lasting forever is slim. Just remember to keep some perspective when you make major decisions.

Do your freaking homework. Yes, it's stupid and unnecessary, but it'll teach you to finish what you start. And let's face it; if you won't do your homework as a kid, you won't do your paperwork as an adult. And then you'll be tracked down by the appropriate authorities and imprisoned. So remember: procrastination and laziness leads to incarceration. Don't be that guy.

Even if you have no interest in what's going on in the class, at least look as though you're paying attention. It'll win you brownie points with the teacher which can be cashed in later, and you might accidentally learn something.

Get to know your teachers. I mean, they are still loosely classified as human, after all. They go places and eat and everything.

Successfully Navigating High School
A Guide for Students Entering High School and Their Parents, Because
the Path to Graduating with Honors Begins in Ninth Grade

CHAPTER 3
SOPHOMORE YEAR
WHAT EVERY PARENT OF A SOPHOMORE AND EVERY SOPHOMORE SHOULD KNOW GOING INTO HIS OR HER SOPHOMORE YEAR.

The SAT

You do not take the SAT this year, you take the PSAT. (You know the test that can identify you as a National Merit Scholar when you take it as a Junior?) This is one of the more important tasks you will accomplish this year. Hopefully you have studied for your PSAT and it will be a good experience for you. You haven't studied? Start now. Right now. You will use the information you gain to help you identify your weaknesses so you can be more successful on the SAT. Part of your homework every weekday night is to spend a few minutes with a few SAT questions. Please don't launch into a "no test should be that important" monologue. It is. Your SAT score will help you to go where you want to go and earn the money it will take to keep you there.

Successfully Navigating High School
A Guide for Students Entering High School and Their Parents, Because
the Path to Graduating with Honors Begins in Ninth Grade

AP or Dual Credit?

Do I really have to decide that now? My child is in a
Pre-AP class. Yes. At the end of the sophomore year, the
student will need to choose to go the regular, on-level
route, the dual credit route, or the advanced placement
route for his junior and senior year. Start thinking now.

The arguments of why and how each is better than the
other are many. Much study and research has been done.
The ground is well covered. The best study I've seen is
the 2009 study completed by the University of Texas at
Austin. You can look it up. I certainly would, but let me
sum it up for you. AP kicks Dual Credit's butt. (That's
my educated paraphrase. I went to college to learn how to
say that.) In all fairness, if you're in the top of your class,
so your acceptance is assured, you're going to a state
school, one in the same state as the dual credit class you
took so that the credit will transfer smoothly, and the dual
credit class you're taking is not in your major field of
study, then it's probably a pretty good deal for you.

Whether it's dual credit or AP, most colleges and
Universities are going to want you to take the classes for
your major field of study at their institution. So if you're
majoring in Engineering, take AP English. If you take AP
Calculus, it's just to learn Calculus, not because you're not
going to have to take the class.

If you're going to college or university out of state, you
need to stick with Advanced Placement.

We won't even mention the International Bache
laureate program, except that I suppose I just did. But
since you asked, if your Daddy is not the ambassador to

Somewhere-scary-a-stan, what is the point? Are there colleges or universities in the US that are not taking high school diplomas now? Good luck with that.

I only have anecdotal evidence. Truthfully, if you need hard data, you can easily look that up. My own child took almost all Pre-AP classes her freshman and sophomore year. By the time she was a junior, she took only the ones for which she could make an A or B. (You can't afford to damage your GPA at this point.) She did not take a test for every class she took. She did not pass every test she took. However, she entered university with 24 credit hours. At about a thousand dollars a credit hour (out of state tuition is brutal) AP was very good to us........I mean her.

Successfully Navigating High School
A Guide for Students Entering High School and Their Parents, Because
the Path to Graduating with Honors Begins in Ninth Grade

The High Cost of a Free Education

Your child's senior year will be one of the most expensive years of his life. As much as you don't think you can afford it, try your very best to begin paying for anything you can now, as you go. Many schools will allow you to pay for your child's senior year beginning in the child's freshman year. You were probably too dizzy from the transition to think about it then. You're settled in now. Start thinking about it seriously. You have: Senior luncheon, Senior trip, Senior fieldtrip, class ring, Senior pictures, announcements, class picture, dances, prom, prom clothing, graduation clothing, graduation cap and gown. If your child has a way to begin paying for events that occur through the school, take advantage of it. You'll be relieved later.

The Love Life

Most high school students don't seem to be able to navigate high school without getting their hearts broken at least once or twice. Maybe it's part of the experience. In three decades of working with high school students, I have seen untold tears in class. Maybe that is just part of the experience, also. I have no advice here. Just expect it. Try to keep it light. Don't be one half of one of those couples who seem determined to swallow one another whole in between classes. Try to remember you're very young, and…. Who am I kidding? Teenagers will fall in love. They always have and they always will. Some will break each other's heart and will cry in every class for a week and learn nothing and some will graduate, marry and live happily together for 70 years. The most self-destructive practice I've seen is that of seniors dating younger students. That a broken heart waiting to happen. One is going to leave and another is going to stay. Wow. What are the odds that this will work out?

I will pass on the sage advice of Gary Rossberg, "Guard your heart." Yes, that's much better advice than I could ever have devised.

Successfully Navigating High School
A Guide for Students Entering High School and Their Parents, Because
the Path to Graduating with Honors Begins in Ninth Grade

THE DRAMA

I wish it were no so, but I cannot tell you have many academic hours are wasted each day dealing with, "He said, She said," or "She said this about me, and now I'm going to…" One of the most vicious fights I've ever seen was between two girls and was over what one of them said about the other on social media. Both girls ended up suspended for three days. What a waste.

I like the advice from one of my former students, Bianca Tesauro who attends the Aveda Institute of Dallas while working many hours,

"Value your relationships with not only your friends, but everyone you come in contact with. Every job you have (unless you plan on being a hermit) will ask you to interact with people. No, they won't all be nice to you, but being smarmy back will only hurt you in the long run. Just be the kind of person you would want to be around."

That's really sound advice, Bianca. If only we all could take it.

Bianca goes on to say,

"Don't take yourself so seriously. After you graduate, you'll realize how petty the drama that circulates the halls really is. Even though it seems like the end of the world now, I promise, it's not. Even if it's the worst it could possibly be, it can only get better. The only opinion you need to value is that of yourself or that of someone you look up to. If you don't want to be like that person, what they think DOES NOT matter. "A lion never loses sleep over the opinions of sheep."

Obviously Bianca has learned some valuable lessons.

Successfully Navigating High School
A Guide for Students Entering High School and Their Parents, Because
the Path to Graduating with Honors Begins in Ninth Grade

The Mistress

As children, one of the first things we learn is that we have very little autonomy. As we grow into our school years, we exercise more and more the ability to make decisions, both good and bad, that reflect in the direction our life goes. The ability to make decisions that then reflect back to life circumstances is a heady power. But soon that is not enough. Soon we want not only power, but freedom. It doesn't take a smart kid to figure out that the most freedom a kid is going to have is having his or her own money to spend and his or her own automobile to drive. For most kids, Sophomore year is the year they hit that magic age of sixteen. That's the year they get to drive. It's what they have been waiting for, longing for. It's also the year in which they may legally work. So what do they do? They get a job, usually in fast food, because those are the people who will hire teenagers. Now they have a little loose change in their pockets and their eyes get big and they begin to lust for the ultimate freedom, their own automobile. Parents, resist the urge to allow your sixteen year old child to get a car payment. It's a vicious cycle. He may at first be able to afford the payment, but cars need more things than just payments. Cars need gas and insurance and oil and repairs and tires and brakes. A car is a greedy, heartless mistress. She may be beautiful and she may call to you, make you lust for her, but she is not worth it. She will drain you dry. She will take everything you have and she will demand more. Resist her.

Here is what happens, over and over and over, Junior gets a job, but gets tired of relying on Mom and Dad for transportation, and hey, he has money now. So, Junior gets a car that he can afford which is often not the best car out there. Junior is still alright, until gas, oil, insurance, repairs, tires, brakes, and so on, so he asks his boss for more hours. Now instead of working for extra money, he is working out of necessity. He has no choices. He must make his payments. He works more hours and he is not getting enough sleep. He is not doing his homework. His teacher says to him, "you must come to tutoring so that you can catch up on your work." Junior says to teacher that he cannot because he must work. He is right. At this point, he must work. My advice to you is not to let your child get to this point, no matter what you have to do. Continue to drive him to work. Don't allow him to get a job. If he is taking the classes that will stand him in good stead as an adult, he doesn't have time for a job now, anyway. But whether you allow him to work or not, unless you his parent can purchase him a car in full, resist the mistress.

Successfully Navigating High School
A Guide for Students Entering High School and Their Parents, Because
the Path to Graduating with Honors Begins in Ninth Grade

CHAPTER 4
JUNIOR YEAR
WHAT EVERY PARENT OF A JUNIOR AND EVERY JUNIOR SHOULD KNOW GOING INTO HIS OR HER JUNIOR YEAR.

CHOOSING THE COLLEGE

Is traditional college the right choice for me?

The junior year is the year parents and students get serious about exactly where they want to go to college. Many skip a very important question, and that is, "Should I go to college?" As an educator, I have to tell you that not everyone can, or even should go to college. We tell our children, "You can be anything you want to be." That's a lie. I am a larger-sized woman. In the past, I have often been frustrated, even hurt by the label claiming that one size fits all. The one size was too small for me. So does that mean I am so far out of the norm that I am not part of the "all?" I feel like an *all*. I want to be an *all*. This is an appropriate analogy in that, like that article of clothing, one size fits most, and to my mind, the label should say that one size fits some. College is like that too. One size fits some.

How do I know if college is for me, for my child? You can answer that yourself by some self- examination, maybe a little reality check. I've had conversations with many students who I asked, "Are you taking advanced classes in English, in math, history, science, language?" From the student I've gotten the response, that no, the advanced classes were not for them. The classes are too much work and require too much homework, are simply too hard. Oh, I say. I will then ask the student his or her plan for after high school. The student will tell me that he or she is planning to go to a major university where he or she plans to embark on a career in business or medicine. This is my puzzled face. AP Biology is too tough, but you are going to be a neuro-surgeon. I have to wonder where these students expect to receive the magic dust that is going to take them from an on-level high school class to a major

Successfully Navigating High School
A Guide for Students Entering High School and Their Parents, Because
the Path to Graduating with Honors Begins in Ninth Grade

university overnight.

Many, many students convince the universities that they will be capable of the transition and off they go to university, with loads of color-coordinated bedding and dorm decorations which end up decorating their bedrooms back home, a semester and thousands of wasted dollars later.

If your child is not in mostly advanced-level high school classes, do not send him or her to a major university as a freshman. Start your student at a junior college. Let him or her see if college is right for him or her. If the harder track in high school was not right for him or her, maybe he or she should explore other options now too. Everyone needs to have some post high school education, but everyone does not need to go to college. Trade schools and the military offer options that are much more realistic for many students. Don't waste two or three precious years after high school trying to make college work for you if it is not right for you. Don't be one of the students who spends three or four years in a two year junior college taking remedial classes, and still not acquiring the skills necessary to take the classes that will count for any degree.

'But my child made all A's in his on-level classes in high school'. Then, in my humble opinion, shame on you, parent. If your child was making A's in on-level classes, then he or she should have been moved into the above level classes.

I have heard many parents say that they really wanted their children to enjoy their senior year of high school, without so many academic demands. That's great. Enjoy! Enjoy the senior year, because your freshman year of college you'll pay for it. Who said, "Eat, drink, and be merry for tomorrow we die!" I need to look that up. Maybe you should too. It seems to be the slogan by which you are planning your child's future.

Successfully Navigating High School
A Guide for Students Entering High School and Their Parents, Because
the Path to Graduating with Honors Begins in Ninth Grade

CHOOSING THE COLLEGE AND EARLY ADMISSIONS

Student, when you choose your college, please do not do so according to which team has the coolest mascot. Do not go to a college because your boyfriend or girlfriend is going there. Take some time to research your future. Make a list of things you're good at that could lead to your possible future vocation, then do some research on colleges and universities that are known for what you are good at. It will be a match worthy of the best internet dating company. Want to stay close to home? Take that into consideration. Need a cheaper route? Certainly that is often a consideration. Make lists. Make lists of your lists. When you are down to your top three choices, consider early admission. I have no scientific data, it is just my observation, but it seems that early admissions are more often successful than later attempts, especially if your GPA and SAT scores are not top flight. If you have a school to which you really want to go, in my estimation, you should submit your admission request on the first day of early admissions. That is earlier and earlier. Which means, you can't begin to think about college admissions at the beginning of your senior year; you must begin to think about college admission at the beginning of your junior year and be ready to take action at the end of your junior year. If you wait until the very beginning of your senior year, you are not too late to go to a very good school, but you may have surrendered the advantage of your top choice to those more prepared.

COLLEGE MAIL

Every fall my seniors come in with piles of brochures they have received from colleges and universities, literally hundreds of them. That they have received this brochure makes them confident that they will be admitted into the college. It's not pretty when the truth begins to sink in. The brochure is an invitation to apply, nothing more. Many times, colleges and universities will send these to everyone who took a PSAT or SAT from a list they purchased for this purpose. They will send out hundreds of thousands of brochures knowing they have only a few hundred, and in some cases, a few thousand seats available. It seems to be the goal to receive thousands of application for every ONE seat available, so that the applications committee may choose the very best applicant. And of course, they must leave room for the college athletes needed to man the various sports on campus.

In short, receiving a brochure is not even close to a guarantee of acceptance, and it doesn't even address how on Earth you are going to pay for it.

CHAPTER 5
SENIOR YEAR
WHAT EVERY PARENT OF A SENIOR
AND EVERY SENIOR SHOULD KNOW
GOING INTO HIS OR HER SENIOR
YEAR.

The College Admissions Essay

The college admissions essay is one that causes knees to knock and nerves to jangle every fall. Don't wait. Start as soon as possible. Early admissions come earlier and earlier.

Your first stop is the website of your chosen colleges and universities. Of course you have a first choice, but you always need a plan B and a plan C. Look at the admissions sites of all three. Do they even require an admission's essay and if they do, do they have a required topic?

Probably they will have a choice of topics. Generally, these topics fall into three categories: the "you," the "why us," and the "creative." Many colleges ask for an essay that will let them know about you. Of course, the essay also allows them to see you as a writer and a potential college student. For this type of essay, you can think of it as a type of lengthy introduction. Think of it being like the kind of introduction given a famous speaker before he takes the dais. This type of essay is often difficult for students. Finding a balance between humility and hubris is hard. You want to tell all the good things about yourself without sounding full of yourself. Yes, very difficult.

Some ask you to tell about an important person in your life. Please, please avoid telling about your boyfriend or girlfriend. The admissions office, as would I, would have to wonder if you will spend your freshman year in relationship dramas, as many do, instead of studying for class. Remember your purpose. You are still telling about yourself, but now you are able to do so in the guise of talking about your significantly influential person. You can

Successfully Navigating High School
A Guide for Students Entering High School and Their Parents, Because
the Path to Graduating with Honors Begins in Ninth Grade

say you learned your strong work ethic from your grandfather which serves to tell you have a strong work ethic without your coming right out and saying it and sounding arrogant.

Please do not tell about how your grandfather helped you to overcome your drug, alcohol, or sex addiction. Telling how your grandfather found you looking at pornography while smoking marijuana at thirteen and convinced you to watch baseball instead may be true, but isn't the sort of information that will have the committee stuffing your inbox with pleas to come to their university. Don't lie. Never lie. It will come back to haunt you. However, there is some information best left unsaid if at all possible.

Some schools will ask for an essay that has you speaking about your choice of career. If you have chosen your career based on its ability to make you rich and your desire to buy your Mom a new house and a diamond ring, choose another essay topic. Your ability to last the long-haul of a college education is going to take more motivation than can be supplied by your avarice. I know it and the admissions office knows it. Further if your desire to make a pile of cash is your sole reason for choosing a profession, think some more. You won't make it.

Some schools want to know, "Why us?" Again, remember the purpose of the essay. Your purpose is to tell what a great student you will be. If the reason you want to attend this university is because you truly admire the quarterback, I suggest you do some research and discover more information about the university so that you can use that information to couch your strong qualities. Still further, if the reason you want to attend a certain university is because of the quarterback, do some more research. Most colleges and universities have pretty talented quarterbacks. You might find a college or university that does really well at the same things that you do really well with, and hey it will be a match made in heaven! If you have not done your research, and do not know the university well, it will become readily apparent to the admissions committee member who is reading your essay. If your mistake is too grievous, your essay will be the one passed around the table for comic relief, before they send you the, "don't call us, we'll call you" letter.

Some colleges evaluate you through your choice of some tangential item: a national issue, a famous person, what you would put in a time capsule, a photograph. Here the school is looking at your creativity and the breadth of your knowledge and education. Be very careful here. We all have very strong views on national issues. I would like to think the person reading your essay would be able to put aside personal feelings and read your essay for its content, but an admissions committee member is still just a human being. Avoid issues with strong emotional tags. Save that for later. You can join a club, or march in a protest. Your college admissions essay is not a great place to make your stand.

Here is the good news, once you have written three or four admissions essays, you are probably set. You can make small changes and use one of these essays for each admissions request and each scholarship application.

Above all, as with all essays, remember your audience and your purpose. Your purpose is to somehow take another step in convincing this committee that if they allow you into their university, you will stay there for four years, pay them a great deal of money, on time, and exit wearing a black robe and mortar board. You will then go out into the world, sing their praises and make regular contributions to the alumni organization. Happy day!

Successfully Navigating High School
A Guide for Students Entering High School and Their Parents, Because
the Path to Graduating with Honors Begins in Ninth Grade

The Educational Resume

At the beginning of your junior year as you begin to narrow your focus and settle on a number of colleges to which you want to apply, you will need to compose your educational resume. You will use this not only for college admissions applications, but also for scholarship applications, internship applications, and many other opportunities that occur during your senior year of high school and your freshman year of college.

Don't "re-invent the wheel." Most word processing programs contain resume templates. Examine your word processor, pc or mac, and determine how it can help you. However, stay away from the resume wizard. It's too confining. In my experience, when you use the wizard, you end of starting over. Use the template. You can change it, maneuver it to your needs.

Typically, the first item on any resume is the objective. On a work force resume, the objective is extremely important, if not most important; however, for an educational resume, the objective is much less important. Keep it entirely general, or remove it altogether.

What's next? On your work force resume, your job experience comes first. On your educational resume, your job experience comes almost last, right before references. Your first title should be EDUCATION. After all, this is your "educational" resume. Begin with high school unless you did something so extraordinary in middle or elementary school that it screams to be included. Did you take a relatively large number of high level classes? List them. You took two? Let's not list the two. You scored really impressively on the SAT? Let's put that on your resume. You scored slightly above someone who spelled his name correctly? Let's not mention your score on the resume. Never lie. But don't purposely put something on your resume that does not speak well of you. In the words of Suzanne Sugarbaker, "If it doesn't look good, don't put it on your front porch!" Good advice, Suzanne!

Next on our resume, we want to include our interests. We want any reader of our resume to see how well rounded and socially healthy we are. Because high school is filled with a myriad of experiences, for this resume "Interests" should be divided into several categories: academic, organizations, extra-curricular activities, volunteer activities and organizations, and community life activities.

Academic organizations are different than Volunteer Organizations. Volunteer Organizations require only that you show up with a willingness to work hard and take an active part. Academic organizations are organizations that you must be invited to join, organizations such as: National Honor Society, Beta Club, National Spanish Honor Society, Mu Alpha Theta, and others that depend on your GPA for admission. Hopefully you have some of both.

The next section is Extra Curricular Activities. This is the place to tell that you are in the band, the drill team, or on the football team. If you made "All-Region" Band three years in a row, list it here. If you were "Miss High Kick" on the drill team, list it here. If you are "Mr. Tenacity" on the football team, list it here.

Then you provide a section for student life activities. If I let you into my university, will you 'work well and play well with others?' If the answer is yes, prove it here. If the answer is no, omit this title altogether. If you were the president of "Tree Huggers United" or even just a member, list it here. Especially if you received awards from that organization, list the awards here. Don't leave anything out, even if you were a member for only a short time in your freshman year. Student Council, Recycling

Successfully Navigating High School
A Guide for Students Entering High School and Their Parents, Because
the Path to Graduating with Honors Begins in Ninth Grade

Team, making mums for handicapped children, this is the place to show what a valuable part of student life you will play if admitted to the university.

Another section you will need is the Community Life Section. This is the category under which you can tell the world that you are an Eagle Scout. Tell how you went with your church youth group to Ecuador three years in a row to build adequate shelter for families. (That is someone I want on my University campus. If you can live in Ecuador, you probably won't grouse about sharing the bathroom with three other people in the dorms.) Tell how you volunteer three hours a weeks to go to the retirement homes to paint the finger nails of elderly ladies.

You're almost finished. The title before the last title is Work Experience. Now it's time to tell how you were shift manager at McDonalds. Tell how you knitted scarves and sold them at the flea market, paying your way to band camp. But remember that this is an academic resume. If you infer that you work 54 hours a week, one will wonder if you will be entirely serious about, or even conscious for, your studies if admitted to a particular university.

It is preferable to put under the "References" label at the bottom of your paper, "References available on request." Then have them available. You should have a list of references, whose names and addresses are neatly typed and copied, ready to give when they are requested of you. However, your references' personal information should never be shared more openly, appearing on every resume. If you cause me to have my identity stolen, your chances of a positive reference have dropped.

Proofread, proofread, proofread. If you've made one mistake, your efforts were for nothing. Your resume will not make a good impression. Choose an easily read font. Cute is for puppies, not for resumes. Look at your resume from a distance. Is it pleasing to the eye? Have you left enough "white space?" Proofread again.

Successfully Navigating High School
A Guide for Students Entering High School and Their Parents, Because
the Path to Graduating with Honors Begins in Ninth Grade

THE FAFSA

The United States Department of Education requires that you fill out the Free Application for Federal Student Aid if you wish to get any Federal Aid. Truly, the first step to paying for college is to fill out the FAFSA. Make sure you go to the official website, not one of the dozens who will fill out your FAFSA for you for a fee. That may sound good, but in order for them to fill out the forms, you will need to give them all the information needed for the forms, and really, by the time you have given the help websites all the information, you could have filled out the official form, for free.

Set aside at least an hour. Sit down at your computer with your tax documents and your patience. Be prepared to follow instructions. There is nothing especially difficult about filling out this on-line document, but it is time consuming. The race goes to the valiant.

Scholarships

How many scholarships did you apply for today? The best school counselor I've ever worked with likes to tell our students, that they must think of applying for scholarships as a part time job.

Spend a couple of hours every day, yes, every day, searching for and completing scholarship applications and then submitting them. Make it your goal to find and apply for one scholarship every day or every other week day. Applying for scholarships is more difficult than you think. Many require essays. Many require projects. Many require paperwork. Again. Think of it as a job, a "must-do" Hard work? Yes. Worth it? Yes.

Successfully Navigating High School
A Guide for Students Entering High School and Their Parents, Because
the Path to Graduating with Honors Begins in Ninth Grade

CHAPTER 6

WHAT EVERY COLLEGE FRESHMAN SHOULD KNOW GOING INTO HIS OR HER FRESHMAN YEAR OF COLLEGE

REINVENT YOURSELF

The great thing about starting college, is that it's a time to begin again. Many students go to another city, even another state for their collegiate experience. They sit next to people they don't know and who don't know them. They could be anybody. So be anybody. If you made mistakes as a freshman in high school, don't make the same mistakes as a freshman in college. Reinvent yourself into what you what to be.

Listen to the words of advice from one of my former students, Katelyn Holliness, "My senior year my AP English teacher, Mrs. Baxter gave my class reassuring advice for college. She allowed us to reflect on our 4 years of high school and told us something I will never forget, "College is your time to reinvent yourself; to start all over". I did not think her words of wisdom would affect me the way it did, but the words Mrs. Baxter spoke followed me all throughout my freshman year of college and still to this day."

Thank you, Katelyn, but it's true. Sometimes mistakes are forever and sometimes you get a 'do-over.'

I've had many students who played on the golf team. I've even watched some professional golf on television. I enjoy it. What I've never heard my competitive students talk about nor heard on the television screen is a Mulligan. A Mulligan is something you get in a friendly game of golf. It's like this. You make a shot and it's awful. It's so awful, you won't be able to play it successfully. Sometimes, when your game is friendly enough, your friends give you a Mulligan. It's a free shot, a start over with no penalty.

College can be like that. When you're a freshman in

Successfully Navigating High School
A Guide for Students Entering High School and Their Parents, Because
the Path to Graduating with Honors Begins in Ninth Grade

college, you get a Mulligan. For heaven's sake, take it.

HOMESICKNESS

How many times have I heard the phrase, "I'm going to leave this peanut town and I'm never coming back, not even on holidays?" Then miraculously, at the first sign of an excuse, behold the parade of the returning, conquering heroes, also known as, last year's seniors returning to campus to just say hello. I always love to see them. I think they may even love to see me, too. And I always know the truth, as much as they thought they would not, they miss home. And you know what? That's OK.

Give yourself permission to feel homesick. It's a completely normal reaction to the transition in your life. Feeling a longing for the past does not mean you don't enjoy your present. You can miss your old friends while you make new ones. You can have both. I give you permission.

One of my former students, Keely Howk, student athlete and Psychology major at Ouachita State University says, "Don't let the fear of not knowing people keep you from trying new things or activities at school because that's where you'll meet great new people. Nothing is better than having good friends to get through college with, especially when finals come and all seems hopeless! Don't worry about not having your friends from high school with you when you go to college because you find your forever best friends at college, and they will get you through anything. Be open to new adventures and new chances. Most importantly for me since I am someone who gets homesick, I would say IT IS OKAY TO CRY!!! Get it all out! But don't worry too much, your family is only a phone call/letter away, and they miss you as much as you miss them!"

That is so true, Keely.

Successfully Navigating High School
A Guide for Students Entering High School and Their Parents, Because
the Path to Graduating with Honors Begins in Ninth Grade

THE MAGIC OF OFFICE HOURS

I've always been pretty hard on my students. When they have a question about a grade or about an assignment that is not the one we are specifically working on today in class, I insist they come to tutorial to talk about their question. Collegiately this is translated into office hours. In most college classes, students are expected to listen and interact about the content in class, but if they have questions about an assignment, this is an appropriate question for office hours only. This can be magical. Office hours can transform you from a name on a piece of paper to a real, live, living, breathing person.

E mail is great stuff too. When you e mail your professor, for the few seconds it takes the professor to answer the e mail, you have all of the professor's attention. One hundred percent. Again, magical!

One of my former students, Eunique Jones, graduated from college in three years, and she had this to say: "Ask questions via email and in person. Sometimes the best way to contact your professor is via email, but many times, personal is better. A face sometimes sticks with a name better than a name on a piece of paper."

Great advice, Eunique. Thank you.

THE STUDY GROUP

In high school, often students get together to study, but what this turns into many times is either a party, or a mass-cheating session. Either is not conducive to good grades. In college, study groups are encouraged. And students are actually expected to study. In the study group. Study. Shocking.

My former student, Eunique Jones has some great advice about this also, she said, "Form reliable study groups. The best way to learn in college is in groups because you're able to absorb more. My Genetics professor told me the magic study group number was three. However, if you feel you need to step out do what you feel comfortable doing."

Thank you, Eunique.

Successfully Navigating High School
A Guide for Students Entering High School and Their Parents, Because
the Path to Graduating with Honors Begins in Ninth Grade

DEFINE YOUR PURPOSE; ARE YOU HERE FOR A PIECE OF PAPER, OR ARE YOU HERE TO LEARN, TO DEVELOP, TO RE-PURPOSE.

Dax Bennington, currently finishing his doctoral work as he serves as a teaching assistant at Texas Tech University, addressed this quite eloquently,

"I think the first thing I would say to students, those entering high school and those entering college, would be to value and get the most out of their educational experience as much as they can. Education is much more than what a professor of mine called intellectual bulimia. This is, memorizing a plethora of irrelevant and unrelated facts and then regurgitating them for the test, never to pay any attention again to the information. Education is the formation of the entire person, heart, mind, and soul. The sooner you begin to realize this, the more you will begin to value and appreciate education. Doing well in school isn't about being able to answer the question, 'How am I going to use this in real life?' but rather, 'How am I being formed through this process?' What sort of person am I becoming?

My professor, David Naugle, would say the purpose of education is to be formed into a good lover, a good thinker, and a good doer. I would concur with him about this and testify that my educational experience dramatically improved once I began to consider not what I was going to do with the information I was learning, but what sort of person I was becoming.

The vision of education starts from day one. Parents play just as much a role in their child's education as do

81

their teachers. The Latin root of education is *educare*, which means to draw out, to rear. It is the parent's role to do this as much as the teachers.

If we do not attend to this vision of education, the consequences will be perilous. As C.S. Lewis writes in the *Abolition of Man*, 'We want men without chests and expect from them virtue and enterprise. We laugh at honor and are shocked to find traitors in our midst.'

To use more Lewisian aphorisms, we create 'trousered apes' and 'urban blockheads.' Nothing less than every effort on the part of both parents and their students will be required to reverse this trend that is occurring."

Dax finishes as he posits that it is the job of every college freshman to think critically, to write clearly and persuasively, and to communicate his or her thoughts articulately.

And to the teachers, Dax presents a challenge, as he again quotes C.S. Lewis, 'The task of the modern educator is not to cut down jungles, but to irrigate deserts.'

Dax, you are a marvel. You took my class, now I want to take yours.

Successfully Navigating High School
A Guide for Students Entering High School and Their Parents, Because
the Path to Graduating with Honors Begins in Ninth Grade

A FINAL THOUGHT

In the introduction of this book I said that one way or another, circumstances will work out in the end and although good choices can make things better, bad choices can eventually be overcome. That is pretty much a lie. I'll confess to you now. I lied. Bad choices as an eighth grader will linger. Bad choices as a high school student may never be totally overcome. I watched a motivational video with my class today about famous people who overcame mediocre starts. They are famous because that almost never happens. Mediocre starts lead to mediocre lives. There's an adage I like to quote by that prolific author, Anonymous, "You will spend your thirties, your forties, your fifties, if you're lucky your sixties and your seventies, and if you're very lucky your eighties and your nineties, reaping the rewards of, or paying the consequences for, the decisions you make between the ages of 14 and 26." The stakes are too high to make a mistake.

TALK TO THE AUTHOR

anitatuckerbaxter@gmail.com

ABOUT THE AUTHOR

Anita Tucker Baxter was born in East Texas.

She now lives in North Texas with her husband, middle daughter and son, and their rescued Chihuahua and Italian Greyhound.
Her oldest daughter is away at college. She misses her every day.

Made in the USA
Monee, IL
05 January 2021